QUICK FIXES

Home Energy
Savings

pil Publications International, Ltd.

Zolton Cohen is a licensed residential building contractor and former ASHI-certified home inspector. "Around the House," his weekly syndicated newspaper column on home repair and home maintenance, is syndicated through Booth Newspapers and also appears online at MLive.com. He lives and works in Kalamazoo, Michigan.

Picture Credits:

Front cover: **Blend Images** (right)

iStockphoto: 10, 43, 44, 55, 59, 75, 80; **PhotoDisc:** 7; **PhotoObjects.net:** 70; **Shutterstock:** 5, 12, 14, 16, 19, 22, 25, 27, 30, 32, 38, 49, 63, 67, 77; **U.S. Environmental Protection Agency, ENERGY STAR Program:** 52

Louis Weber, CEO
Publications International, Ltd.
7373 North Cicero Avenue
Lincolnwood, Illinois 60712

ISBN-13: 978-1-4127-8260-9
ISBN-10: 1-4127-8260-0

Manufactured in U.S.A.

8 7 6 5 4 3 2 1

CONTENTS

USE ENERGY WISELY

We have lived in an age when relatively inexpensive energy has improved the quality of our lives to a degree undreamed of by our ancestors. But the "relatively inexpensive" part of that equation is changing. All forms of the energy we use in our homes have been rising in price. While there's not much we can do about what utility companies charge for the energy they provide, there are usually quite a few things we can do to reduce our use of energy— and, therefore, our monthly household utility bills.

Saving money is not the only reason to conserve energy. Concerns over the consumption of finite energy resources and our individual "carbon footprint" should alert us to our responsibility for the amount of greenhouse gasses produced by our activities and should make us all the more aware of our impact on the environment. From the extraction and burning of coal, oil, and gas to the generation of electricity, creating energy is a dirty business. As home-owners and citizens of a country and a planet, we all would be better off using less energy. This book can help us with that vital goal.

Quick Fixes: Home Energy Savings contains simple, useful tips on how to reduce energy consumption in our homes. Many of the techniques described in these chapters can be put into practice without investing any money or time. The idea is to change the way we think about energy use and conservation. If we take the time and energy to implement some of these strategies, the result should be lower energy bills, as well as a reduction of our carbon footprint. We'll be doing our part for the environment and saving money at the same time.

Chapter One, "Energy-Efficient Living," covers ways we can modify some of the things we do and the way we live in our houses in order to conserve energy.

Chapter Two, "Increase Energy Efficiency," offers ways to improve energy efficiency in our homes by altering or manipulating some of the existing energy-using devices, appliances, and equipment. These tips might require a few skills to implement and may require a small investment in materials and time.

Chapter Three, "Get Your Hands Dirty," contains important information about how improving air sealing, insulation, and weather stripping can provide incredible energy savings whether we do the work ourselves or hire a competent professional.

Chapter Four, "Make Improvements Around the House," details how upgrading some of the equipment in a home, such as the furnace, boiler, air-conditioning system, or appliances, can have a big effect on the energy bill. This chapter also talks about why investing in some of the new technology on the market makes sense. It gives insight into some of the recent energy-saving developments in the fields of heating, air conditioning, lighting, and window replacement. If nothing else, the information provides terminology and an understanding that may help a homeowner talk

knowledgeably with a contractor doing certain types of energy-upgrading work.

Chapter Five, "Consider Whole-House Issues," deals with health and safety concerns that may come into play as a home is weatherized. It answers the question of whether or not it is possible to make a house "too airtight." Also included is information about ice dam formation on rooftops in the winter: a symptom of an energy-inefficient home.

In reading this book, we'll discover the many benefits of thoughtful, intelligent, and reduced use of energy. The less energy each of us uses means that less energy needs to be generated. And fewer power plants that need to be built means the less they need to run. Our country's dependence on foreign oil supplies can be cut back, and we can stretch existing supplies of coal, oil, and natural gas so that our children and grandchildren can live their lives in comfort, similar to what we have enjoyed, without paying a hefty price.

It might seem that some of the tiny, incremental steps toward energy conservation suggested in these pages can't mean much in the overall scheme of things. But as a Chinese proverb tells us, "A journey of a thousand miles begins with a single step." All those individual steps add up over time. Multiplied by the millions of homes in this country, even a slight reduction in personal energy-usage habits can result in significant conservation of our nation's energy supplies.

Similarly, the multiple small steps toward energy conservation we take in our homes will result in lower energy bills. While some of the tips in these chapters might seem inconsequential, added together they can have a surprising—and pleasing—effect on the bottom line of the monthly utility bill. Multiplied over the course of a year, these "thousand steps" can help achieve better energy efficiency. And that adds up to real savings—in more ways than one.

CHAPTER ONE

ENERGY-EFFICIENT LIVING

How we choose to live in our homes every day affects our energy consumption. This chapter of the *Quick Fixes: Home Energy Savings* contains tips on ways we can reduce that consumption by simply altering the way we do some everyday things.

HEATING AND COOLING

Dial Down the Thermostat in Winter

Space heating constitutes the largest energy expenditure in many homes, so conserving even a little of the fuel you use to heat your home can go a long way toward achieving a lower utility bill. During the day, dialing down the thermostat even one degree can result in 1 to 3 percent less fuel use, as well as a similar reduction in the heating bill.

A furnace or boiler must maintain a differential in temperature between the inside of the house and the outdoors in order for the house to feel comfortable. On cold days that difference can be as much as 50–60 degrees (say, 20 outside and 70 inside). If the differential can be reduced, even by a degree or two, the heating system comes on less often, less fuel is burned, and savings result.

Increase Personal Insulation

The downside of turning down a thermostat is that the house will be cooler. But instead of turning up the heat to increase the overall warmth in the big volume of space

WHAT'S A BTU?

Furnaces, boilers, air conditioners, kitchen ranges, and water heaters are all classified by their BTU output. But what is a "BTU"?

BTU stands for British Thermal Unit. One BTU is the amount of heat it takes to raise one pound of water one degree Fahrenheit. The burners in ranges, water heaters, boilers, and furnaces are rated by the amount of BTUs they can produce per hour.

A conventional storage-type gas water heater might have a burner rated at 35,000 or 40,000 BTUs. Forced-air gas furnaces, depending on size, might range from 25,000 up to 150,000 BTUs.

The "heat load" or cooling load on your house is calculated in BTUs, too. Wall and floor construction, wall and ceiling insulation, size of the house, number of windows, typical outdoor temperatures, and other factors are evaluated to determine how much heat or cooling in BTUs the house will lose per hour. Your heating and cooling equipment is sized to accommodate the BTU loss based on these calculations.

inside the house, simply increase personal insulation by putting on warmer clothing to help retain body heat. Though dialing down might seem a hardship at first, after a while our bodies adjust to the "new normal" house temperature, and wearing sweaters and socks inside will become a part of everyday life.

Save More at Night and While the House Is Unoccupied

To increase heating fuel savings at night and when the house is unoccupied, reduce the thermostat's setting even further. Some people prefer to "sleep cold," and don't mind turning down the thermostat to the low 60s or high 50s at night. Those who are comfortable dialing down this far are able to reduce heating fuel consumption substantially. For those who desire similar savings but don't think they could tolerate the cold, it is possible to stay warm under the covers even while dialing down. Down or synthetic-filled comforters provide insulation with little weight; an electric blanket generates warmth at a small cost in electrical energy.

Dial Up the Thermostat in Summer

"Dialing up" is an effective method of reducing the cost of cooling a house with room or central air conditioning. The same principles explained in lowering heating costs apply: The less the temperature differential between the inside and outside the air-conditioning system has to maintain, the less often the compressor comes on, the less electricity is consumed, and the lower the utility bill.

Instead of setting the thermostat to the point that the air-conditioning system makes the house cold, dial up a few degrees and adjust clothing to deal with the slightly warmer temperature. Chances are the difference won't be noticeable. And, as is the case with heating, dialing up the thermostat when the house isn't occupied results in lower energy consumption.

Heat Less Space

If there are rooms in the house that aren't being used, shutting the doors and vents to those rooms results in a reduction in the volume of area that the heating and air-conditioning systems have to heat and cool. If a child moves away from home or parts of the basement aren't being used, isolating those areas from the rest of the house means less demand in terms of heating and cooling, as well as a lower energy bill.

HOME ENERGY MANAGEMENT AND CONTROL

Actively "managing" a house to take advantage of or to exclude natural energy sources can reduce the burden on heating and air-conditioning systems and result in energy savings.

Use Free Passive Solar Heat in the Winter

In the winter, opening up shades and drapes on south-facing windows allows sunlight inside the house so it can warm floors, furniture, and furnishings. During the winter, the sun is lower on the horizon, so sunlight penetrates deeper into the house than it does when almost directly overhead in the summer. Utilizing this "passive solar" heating on a sunny day can reduce the number of times your heating system has to activate.

Prevent Heat Loss Through Windows at Night

During a winter night, heavy or insulating shades and drapes drawn over the windows will keep heat inside, acting as both a radiant heat barrier for heat leaving the home and also as insulation over the cold window glazing.

Exclude Solar Heat Gain in Summer

During the summer, closing shades and drapes will keep the warming rays of sunlight out of the house, reducing the load on the cooling system.

Use Fans to Avoid Having Air Conditioning Turn On

Employing a time-honored strategy—getting the air to move—reduces the use of central or room air conditioning. It's cheaper to operate simple desktop or standing fans, which make the air seem cooler by several degrees by evaporating moisture from the skin, than to use the A/C.

DO CEILING FANS COOL A ROOM WHEN IT IS UNOCCUPIED?

No, ceiling fans do not create cool air in a room. The air passing over your skin has a "wind chill" effect that makes you feel cooler, but the air itself does not decrease in temperature. In fact, since an electrical motor powers a ceiling fan, the motor actually creates a little bit of heat when the ceiling fan is operating.

Using ceiling fans, however, is a good way to limit the amount of time an air-conditioning system has to run in the summer. And it's best to use them only when there are people in the room to enjoy the effects of the passing air and to turn them off when the occupants depart.

Those without ceiling fans but with a forced-air furnace have the option of switching on the furnace's blower fan to help move warm and stagnant air. Most thermostats have a setting called "on" between "off" and "auto." Flipping the switch to "on" causes the fan to run continuously. Running the furnace blower fan for a few hours every day reduces the need for operating an air-conditioning system and thus saves money.

Use Ceiling Fans Instead of A/C

Ceiling fans are also quite useful. They draw up and distribute cooler air that lies along the floor, gently moving all of the air in a room at once. Nevertheless, because neither ceiling nor portable fans make the air itself cool, running them when no one is in the room is a waste of energy.

Shut Off Lights

The simple act of turning off lights when leaving a room saves energy. An urban myth says turning on a light uses more energy than it consumes while it is operating. It is true that when an incandescent or fluorescent lightbulb is first switched on, it requires a brief surge of electricity. But the electricity consumed during start-up is equivalent to only a few seconds' worth of running the light. So keep bulbs that aren't being used turned off.

ENERGY-EFFICIENT KITCHEN PRACTICES

Use Smaller Appliances to Cook

In the winter, firing up a gas or electric oven or range contributes to the heat needed to keep the house warm—a benefit. That heat is unwelcome in the summer, because the air-conditioning system is called upon to remove the heat and dump it outside the house. Therefore, during summer, conventional cooking practices are doubly inefficient; they generate unneeded heat, and then the A/C has to come on to remove it from the house.

Baking a few potatoes or other small food items can be accomplished quickly and at much less energy cost in a microwave oven than a conventional oven. Countertop toaster ovens and broilers can prepare a wide variety of foods, and they don't produce the amount of heat or consume nearly the energy used by a full-size range.

Combine Cooking Tasks and Shut Off Burners Early

If using an oven, simultaneously cook foods that require similar temperatures. Using lids on pots on the range prevents heat from escaping and reduces cooking time.

Shut off ovens and range-top burners before the food is completely cooked, allowing the food to "coast" until done.

Use the Range Hood to Save Energy

Range hoods that vent outdoors help remove cooking odors, humidity, heat, and combustion by-products generated by gas ranges and ovens. Using the range hood in the summer lowers the load on air conditioning by expelling heat produced by cooking to the outdoors. "Recirculating" range hoods do not remove heat or pollutants and are only marginally effective at straining humidity and odors from the air.

Cook Big Batches

Cooking large batches of food makes sense for time management and energy conservation reasons. Volume cooking of soups, stews, and spaghetti sauce, and then freezing the extras for later use, makes the best use of cooking fuel.

Use the Refrigerator Wisely

To minimize cooling loss, open the refrigerator door once to remove all the food needed at any one time. Allow warm foods to cool to room temperature before moving them to the refrigerator.

Turn Off the Refrigerator Condensation Control Switch

Most newer refrigerators incorporate small heating elements in the main cabinet near the door. Heat from the elements prevents condensation in this narrow, hard-to-insulate area. Continual condensation wetness in the summer encourages mildew and mold growth. In the winter, the auxiliary heat is usually not required in the drier indoor air, so the electricity the heaters draw goes to waste. There is a control box in refrigerators equipped with these heating elements, and the switch that controls the elements can be turned off for much of the year.

Wash Dishes by Hand

Domestic water heating makes up nearly a quarter of the typical family's utility bill, but intelligent use of hot water while dishwashing by hand can reduce that by a significant amount. Running water constantly while washing dishes wastes not only water but also the energy required to heat it.

Close up the drain and run a couple of inches of hot water in the bottom of a sink, along with some liquid dish detergent. Turn off the faucet. Wash glasses, cups, and silverware in this soap-concentrated water, and rinse off the soap over the same sink filled with water. The hot water used for rinsing runs into the sink, filling it up further for the larger items to come. The soap used to wash these first items is retained as well.

Stack plates in the soapy water and wash them. Remove each plate as it is washed, and stack it in the bottom of the adjacent empty sink. When a good pile has accumulated, run water over the stack and remove and rinse each plate in turn. Water running from the plates as they are removed helps do a preliminary rinse on the next plate below, doing "double duty" on its way down the drain.

When everything has been washed, don't drain the wash water out of the sink. Let the water's heat help warm and

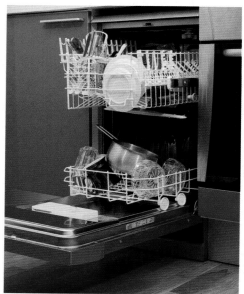

humidify the room. In the summer, drain the hot water quickly in order to avoid adding its heat to the air-conditioning load.

Using an Automatic Dishwasher

Do not rinse dishes before adding them to a dishwasher. That wastes water and the energy to heat it. Newer dishwashers are equipped with sensors that determine how long the wash cycle runs in order to get dishes clean. The sensors detect food particles in the wash water. As long as the sensors "see" food particles in the wash water, the wash cycle will continue. Rinsing dishes before loading fools the internal sensors into believing the wash cycle is nearly complete before it has had time to work. With few food particles to sense, the cycle switches almost immediately to rinse. The result can be dirty dishes.

Shut off the rapid dry feature on the dishwasher and let the dishes air-dry. Using electrical energy to dry the dishes is unnecessary and wasteful.

ENERGY-EFFICIENT LAUNDRY ROOM PRACTICES

Wash Clothes in Cold Water

Use cold water rather than hot water for washing clothes—the hot water heater will get a rest, and the clothes come out just as clean. In areas where the water entering the home during the winter is cold, liquid detergent works better than a powder. Most powders do not dissolve as well in cold water as they do in warm.

For both water and energy savings, do full loads of laundry whenever possible. Running a washing machine to do one large load as opposed to several smaller ones uses less electricity to power the machine's motor, and overall water consumption will be lower as well. Letting laundry stack up a bit is not a sign of laziness; it's saving energy.

Use a Dryer Sensibly

To minimize the energy used to dry clothing, use the automatic-drying feature on the dryer. Set on "automatic," a sensor in the drum measures the amount of moisture in the air exiting the dryer. Once the moisture level in that air is reduced to an acceptable level the dryer shuts off. No more gas or electricity is used than is necessary to dry a load of clothes. A "timed" dryer cycle keeps heating and tumbling clothes even after they are dry, until the set time is finished. Not only does this waste energy, but it also unnecessarily heats and wears down the clothes, shortening their life.

Hang Clothing Outside to Dry

Heat used to tumble clothes dry is produced by electricity or natural or propane gas. Avoid using any energy at all to dry clothes by letting the sun and wind do the job. Clotheslines and folding dryers are inexpensive, and it takes only a few minutes to hang a load of wash outdoors.

Using a clothes dryer also ages and deteriorates clothing. High heat breaks down material fibers and causes them to fracture and loosen. The tumbling action of clothing rubbing against other clothing is also abrasive, further deteriorating the material. Thus drying on an outside line pays off not only in terms of energy efficiency but also in clothing longevity.

Hang Clothing Indoors in the Winter

An alternative to hanging clothing outside in the winter is to set up a place inside for drying, usually in the basement. If the house is dry during the winter, the evaporating water from the drying clothes adds welcome moisture to the air. In homes that already have adequate humidity, however, adding more moisture can bring on problems like condensation on walls and ceilings and subsequent mildew and mold growth.

ENERGY-EFFICIENT BATHROOM PRACTICES

Schedule Bathroom Tasks to Use Less Hot Water

Brushing teeth before proceeding to face washing can save hot water. It usually takes a while for hot water to make its way to a bathroom when the tap is opened. Therefore, use the hot water tap first to provide water for brushing teeth. By using the cold water that is resting in the hot water pipe to brush teeth, the time it takes for hot water to reach the fixture for face washing is reduced.

Shorter Showers and Baths Save

By shortening the length of showers, savings can be realized on hot water and the energy required for heating it. Many modern showerheads are equipped with a simple shut-off valve located at the nozzle that allows for turning the flow of water on and off without affecting the temperature setting. Rinsing, shutting the water off while lathering up, and then turning it back on to rinse the soap off will yield much less hot water use.

Filling a bathtub an inch or two lower is unlikely to make any difference from a hygiene standpoint, and the water and energy saved add up. Also, consider taking a shower instead of a bath in the first place. A shower, if it's kept to a reasonable length, usually requires less water than a bath.

Leave the Water in the Tub

When finished in the bath, leave the water in the tub for a few hours. The heat retained in the water adds some heat to the bathroom. Additionally, in a dry house during the winter, the bathwater will add some needed humidity to the air. Do the opposite during the summer. The sooner the bathwater runs out of the tub the better. That way it won't add its heat and moisture to the air.

CHAPTER TWO

INCREASE ENERGY EFFICIENCY

Homeowners can make plenty of no-cost or low-cost alterations to devices, appliances, and equipment that already exist in the home to increase their energy efficiency.

WINDOWS

Lock Windows

Most windows, both casement and double-hung types, are made with compressible weather stripping that helps seal out air infiltration along the edges and between the upper and lower sash. The locks on casement windows draw the sash closer to the frame, compressing the weather stripping and creating a more airtight seal.

Sash locks on double hung windows bring the upper and lower sashes closer together in the middle, compressing the weather stripping located there. The locks also prevent the upper sash from sliding down and the lower one from moving up, which can compromise the weather strip seal on the upper window jamb and lower sill.

WATER HEATERS

Lower Water Heater Temperature Setting

The cost of heating water for domestic use may amount to as much as 15–20 percent of a home's entire utility bill. Setting a water heater's thermostat to the 130-degree range means the water heater uses minimal energy to heat and hold the water at that temperature. Every 10 degrees dialed down on the thermostat from a higher setting can knock 3–5 percent off the cost of the energy used to heat water.

In addition, a lower hot water temperature reduces the chance of scalding.

Setting the thermostat to 130 degrees should produce 120-degree water at the tap, due to heat loss in the piping between the water heater and the fixtures where the water is used. That's low enough to prevent injury but still hot enough to produce a satisfyingly warm shower or bath. Moreover, 130 degrees is also sufficiently hot to prevent bacteria from growing inside the water heater's tank.

Water Heater Temperature Adjustments

Gas and oil water heaters can be adjusted by turning the dial thermostat on the front of the control box. There may be degree markings on the dial, but many only have simple arrows that point the direction to "hot" and "not-so-hot" settings. Gradually dialing down over the course of several days will eventually yield a temperature that is comfortable.

Adjusting the temperature setting on an electric water heater is more complicated and requires removing coverings over the heating elements, which should be attempted only after the power to the unit has been turned off. Small screws attached to the heating elements can be turned to the desired temperature. Most have painted or engraved temperature reading marks on the screw housing. Both heating elements must be dialed to the same degree reading or one might never activate. Check the owner's manual before adjusting the temperature of an electric water heater to follow safety procedures.

Dialing Down Extends Water Heater's Service Life

There are other good reasons to dial down a water heater's thermostat. High water temperatures can contribute to early failure of the tank. Because chemical reactions occur more quickly in hotter environments, rusting of the steel tank is accelerated under high temperature conditions. Plus, sediment (hard-water minerals) precipitates out of hard water more rapidly. It collects at the tank's bottom and reduces the energy efficiency of the water heater.

THERMOSTAT

"Setback" of Heating and Cooling System

As discussed in Chapter One, dialing down the house temperature a few degrees during a home's occupied hours is helpful in terms of energy conservation. But it is at night and when the house is unoccupied that the thermostat setting can be lowered even more, significantly reducing energy consumption.

HVAC experts estimate that every degree the thermostat is dialed down (or up, in the summer) saves 1–3 percent on a home's heating or cooling utility bill. That can yield considerable savings when the many hours a home's occupants spend either in bed or away are taken into account.

The question often arises, "How long does the thermostat have to remain at a low setting in order to save enough energy to make up for what it takes to get the house back up to temperature when the heat is dialed back up?" The answer is that the energy savings during the period when the house temperature falls immediately after the thermostat is dialed down are cancelled out as the furnace works to bring the house back up to temperature after the thermostat is dialed back up. So those two time periods even out.

DEGREE DAYS

Heating and cooling contractors use "degree days" as a mathematical tool to help determine how much energy you could save by upgrading to higher efficiency HVAC equipment. There are two types of degree days: heating degree days and cooling degree days.

Heating degree days are calculated by adding the warmest and the coldest temperature recorded in an area during a 24-hour period. That sum is divided by two and then subtracted from 65 degrees. Each degree of temperature below 65 is called one degree day.

Cooling degree days are calculated the same way, except that once you've determined your average temperature, you subtract 65 from that number, instead of vice versa. Thus, any degrees of temperature above 65 degrees in the final sum are counted as cooling degree days. Homeowners who live in areas with a high number of heating degree days receive a faster payback on an investment in energy-efficient heating equipment than those who live in areas with lower numbers of heating degree days. Conversely, homeowners who live in areas with a high number of cooling degree days benefit from faster payback on energy-efficient cooling equipment than those who live in colder climates.

The savings lie during any hours spent with the thermostat set at the lower temperature. The furnace comes on less frequently as it is asked to maintain a smaller temperature differential between the indoors and outdoors. And the lower the thermostat is dialed, the more savings are realized.

Using a Digital Thermostat

Many programmable, digital thermostats on the market can assist periodic dialing down—or temperature "setback." An investment of $40 to $100 buys a thermostat that can be programmed to automatically dial down the heat at a certain time at night or when the house is unoccupied and turn it back up again as morning arrives or when someone is due home. The automated features of a digital thermostat eliminate having to remember to manually dial up or down. They also ensure that residents wake up to a house that is up to its normal temperature in the morning.

Greater Precision Saves Energy, Increases Comfort

Digital thermostats are also more accurate than older-style mercury switch units; they can differentiate room temperature down to a fraction of a degree. This results in more exacting control of the HVAC system, eliminating large temperature swings and delivering better comfort—as well as energy savings from the setback function. The programming features also help in the summer when setting the thermostat to allow the temperature to rise in the house while it is unoccupied (in order to avoid having the A/C come on as often).

Costlier digital thermostats offer more flexibility and the ability to retain more diverse scheduling; less expensive units are more limited in the scope of their programs. Some higher-end models have the ability to program different setback and wake-up settings separately for every day of the week. This can be helpful for those who need to rise at different times on different days.

All digital thermostats can be overridden at any time to accommodate a specific need, such as cooling a house full of people during a summer party.

Several types of digital thermostats are available to fit different configurations of HVAC systems. The thermostat must fit the system in order to work properly.

If an old thermostat is replaced with a digital model that has a mercury switch (look for a small glass vial inside that holds a silvery liquid), it must be handled carefully to avoid breakage, and it must be disposed of properly. Mercury is a toxin and an environmental hazard. If the manufacturer of the new thermostat doesn't directly participate in a recycling program, take the old thermostat to the nearest hazardous material recycling center.

Manual Thermostat Setback

An unsophisticated, manual-type thermostat can still provide setback functions; it simply needs to be turned down every night and dialed back up again in the morning. One drawback to a manual thermostat is that the house will be cool in the morning before the furnace raises it to the desired temperature.

For many people, setting a manual thermostat up or down as they leave and enter the house, or go to bed and wake up, becomes an easily-remembered habit. For others, the automated setback features offered by a digital thermostat make that option more convenient. Digital or manual, the key point is that any time the thermostat is turned down in the winter or turned up in the summer energy consumption is reduced.

FANS

Whole House Fan Issues

Many homes in the United States have large "whole house" fans mounted in a top-floor ceiling. Homeowners often use them in the summer as an alternative to employing a central or room air conditioner.

Whole house fans bring outside air in through open windows, while at the same time pushing warm air out through the attic and roof vents. The air movement removes heated air from the attic, which can reduce the heat in the rooms below. And if the incoming air is cool, the system does have a cooling effect on the house and its occupants. Whole house fans can also quickly vent undesirable odors when necessary.

Air from outside the house, however, also brings with it humidity, pollen, and dirt. That may limit the use of whole house fans in areas that experience high humidity in the summer or when there is dust or pollen in the air.

Conditioned Air Loss Through a Whole House Fan

Many conventional whole house fan installations lack adequate provision for sealing and insulating the opening in the winter. Loose-fitting metal louvers under a whole house fan allow heated air to escape the house and enter the attic, resulting in energy waste and higher heating bills. In the summer, heat from the attic can also be conducted downward through the opening and the louvers.

Although a whole house fan may save some energy during the summer by prolonging the periods when a room or central air-conditioning system doesn't run, it wastes energy in the winter by allowing warm air to flow upward through the louvers. That opening in the ceiling—one of the largest and potentially leakiest holes in the entire house—substantially increases energy consumption. Draping a length of fiberglass batt insulation over the fan in the winter—a common practice undertaken to address this issue—is completely ineffective as either an air-sealing or an insulating measure.

Remediation of Whole House Fans

Several types of commercially available covers are designed to address air leakage through whole house fans. Some mount on top of the fan in the attic; others are simple covers that attach to the louvers. It is also relatively easy to build a lightweight removable cover of fiberglass insulation board or rigid foam board. Sealing these covers is challenging, but it is critical to preventing air infiltration and exfiltration.

Whole House Fan Alternatives

An alternative to large, conventional whole house fans are smaller fans that have spring-loaded, insulated covers that snap tightly into place when the fan is not being used. While they do not move as much air as the larger models, they are effective if used over longer periods. They also use less power, seal and insulate better, and are quieter, and the hole they require in the ceiling is smaller than that needed for a conventional unit.

FIREPLACE

Close Up a Fireplace Fluepipe

In a home with a fireplace, there is a large hole that leads directly to the outside. That hole is the fireplace flue. Through this opening heated and cooled air escape the house.

Wood-burning fireplaces usually have a damper installed in the upper part of the firebox. The damper is designed to be shut when the fireplace is not in use and can be easily opened when it is. It is common to forget to close the damper after a fire goes out, and that leaves an unobstructed opening right to the outdoors.

Better Fireplace Air Sealing

Even when a fireplace damper is closed, the sealing is often not effective. Adding glass doors to the front of the fireplace can significantly improve the installation's airtightness, as can a "top-sealing damper." Top-sealing dampers fit on top of the flue on the chimney and are controlled by pulling on a cable that hangs inside the fireplace's firebox.

There are also commercially made chimney "balloons" available that can be inflated inside the firebox to seal off the opening at the bottom of the flue. Sealing a fireplace flue in this manner can also reduce or eliminate soot odors that are prone to travel into the house during windy or stormy days. The blocking material must be removed before a fire is started.

A cautionary note: A wood-burning fire must be completely out and the ashes cold before the damper can be shut or other sealing is put into place. A smoldering fire, even though it might not be visible through a layer of ashes, still produces carbon monoxide. Do not close a fireplace damper until the fire is completely out.

Shut Off the Pilot in a Gas-Log Fireplace

Gas-log fireplaces are equipped with either a standing pilot light (one that is lit all the time) or with an electronic ignition. Electronic-ignition models are much more energy efficient because they eliminate the standing pilot flame.

Pilot lights in gas-log fireplaces can be shut off—at least during the summer months. Instructions on how to shut off and relight gas-log pilot lights are printed inside the front panel of most installations or are available from the installer or manufacturer.

Gas-Log Fireplace Damper Issues

Gas-log fireplaces are required to have a keep-open device attached to the damper. The device will not allow the damper to shut. The flames in a gas-log fireplace—both the pilot and the fire when it is turned on—produce carbon monoxide. The always-open damper ensures that the carbon monoxide and other combustion by-products vent outside in a fail-safe manner.

Unfortunately, the open damper means either warm house air is escaping up the flue or cold air might be traveling down the flue.

LIGHTBULBS

Swap Incandescent Lightbulbs for Compact Fluorescent Bulbs

Electricity consumed for lighting typically constitutes nearly 10 percent of the household energy budget. One way to reduce that number is to replace incandescent lights with compact fluorescent light (CFL) bulbs. CFLs use about one third the power required to produce the same amount of light emitted by a standard incandescent bulb. A 13-watt model can replicate the light produced by a 60-watt incandescent; a savings of 47 watts per hour of operation. Multiplied by the number of lights in the average home and their hours of operation, the savings add up quickly.

CFLs offer other advantages, too. Incandescents give off a substantial amount of heat. That heat, while welcome in the winter, adds to the cooling load during the summer. CFLs run cool. They don't contribute to heating load and can be used safely in any fixture that can handle an incandescent—except those controlled by a dimmer switch.

Newer CFLs Are Less Expensive, Produce Better Light

New versions of CFLs mimic the light color given off by incandescent bulbs. Their electronic ballasts produce flicker-free and noiseless light. The bulbs start right up when switched on—though they may require a few minutes to achieve full brightness. New CFL bulb shapes mean CFLs can go anywhere an incandescent fits; the bulb shapes have become more compact and "standard-size" over the years.

The price of CFLs continues to fall. In multipacks and on sale, they cost little more than incandescent bulbs, yet are rated to last 10,000 hours compared to an incandescent's service life of 800–11,000.

One caveat about CFLs; they contain mercury and need to be disposed of in a hazardous waste facility to prevent pollution of water supplies.

Halogen Lights Are Not Energy-Savers

Halogen lights require slightly less electricity to operate than standard incandescent bulbs. Some, however, require transformers that suck up power even when the bulbs are turned off (see the information about standby power on page 30).

Halogens also produce a prodigious amount of heat. They become so hot that they can be fire and burn hazards if installed or used improperly. During the summer that extra heat output is unwelcome and causes air conditioning to run more often.

LEDs, the Next Generation of Energy Saving Lightbulbs

Light emitting diode (LED) lights are just beginning to transform the way we will light our homes and businesses in the future. These bulbs produce very little heat, are rated to last 100,000 hours, and are highly efficient—as much as 80–90 percent more efficient than incandescent bulbs. As manufacturing prices drop, these bulbs will be showing up on more store shelves in the future.

Daylighting—Light Tubes Provide Free Light

To cut down on the amount of energy consumed for lighting tasks and increase the use of daylight for illumination, new products on the market— "light tubes," "sun tubes," or "tubular skylights"—offer many of the benefits of skylights but at lower cost.

LED HOLIDAY LIGHTING

You can take advantage of LED technology today in the form of holiday lighting strings. Although LEDs produce a brilliant white light, the bulbs can also be made with colored glass in order to produce different tints. They are available at many hardware stores and home centers. Due to their popularity, however, many places sell out their stock before the holidays.

If your electricity bill skyrockets over the Christmas season due to the use of holiday lighting, consider investing in LED lighting strings to reduce your electrical consumption.

Light tubes consist of a flexible metal tube that connects a light-gathering dome on the roof and a light-emitting dome inside the house. Daylight hits the exterior dome and is beamed inside the shiny tube. It bounces around inside the tube and comes out through the ceiling-mounted dome. On bright days a light tube can produce more light than a 100-watt bulb.

Because of their modest size and flexibility, light tubes can be installed between standard framing members, requiring no cutting (and thus no resupporting) of those members. The dome that mounts on the roof is supplied with flashing that integrates with the existing roofing, and the interior dome mounts in a simple hole cut into the ceiling. Because light tubes are not as large as most skylights, the heat loss at night is less by comparison.

Light tubes work only during daylight hours (and not as well on cloudy days), but some brands offer optional light fixtures inside so the dome can be used at any time of the day or night.

ELECTRICAL DEVICES

Standby Power Losses

Many electronic devices consume electricity 24 hours a day just to stay warmed up for whenever we decide to use them. The result is "standby" power loss. Energy experts estimate that approximately 5 percent of residential electrical power consumption in the United States is used for standby power.

TV sets, microwave ovens, battery chargers, computers, computer monitors, VCRs, DVD players, and cable TV and satellite TV boxes all use standby power. Some use large, plug-in transformers to step down power, for example to cordless phones and answering machines.

In a typical home, the six to ten devices that use standby power only consume 3–5 watts each. But multiplied by 24-hour days for a year, the standby power loss is significant.

Use Power Strips to Shut Off Standby Power

One way to deal with standby power losses is to plug several devices into a single power strip equipped with an on/off switch. An entire cluster of items can then be shut off—really shut off—just by flicking one switch. Power strips are inexpensive and available at home centers and office supply stores.

Power strips work well in areas like home entertainment centers, where a TV, VCR, DVD player, game box, and cable box might already be plugged into one electrical receptacle. This solution, however, won't work when one of the devices is set to record a TV program or when

the appliance has a clock feature on which the household depends to tell time.

Set a Proper Refrigerator and Freezer Temperature

A refrigerator set to an improper temperature wastes electricity and can cause food spoilage. Refrigerator and freezer temperatures can be set using an accurate thermometer and the easy-to-find controls inside the refrigerator compartment.

Set the refrigerator to 36 to 38 degrees, and the freezer to 0 to +5 Fahrenheit. Food won't last any longer if it is kept at a lower temperature, and some items, such as lettuce and other vegetables, can even freeze and be destroyed by lower temperatures in the refrigerator compartment.

Use a Dehumidifier Correctly to Save Energy

Because a portable dehumidifier uses quite a bit of electricity, having it run as infrequently as possible will result in less energy consumption.

Dehumidifiers are controlled by a humidistat. As the humidity in the area where the dehumidifier is located drops to a certain setpoint, the humidistat shuts off the machine until the humidity rises past that setpoint again, at which time the humidistat turns the dehumidifier back on.

Turning the humidistat to its lowest setting causes a dehumidifier to run constantly, which is wasteful. Find a comfortable humidity reading and set the humidistat to that level. The unit will run intermittently, saving energy compared to letting it run continuously.

Space Heaters and Room Air Conditioners Can Save Energy If Used Appropriately

The adjustment to a cooler house in the winter and a warmer one in the summer can be aided by the use of

devices designed to increase personal comfort. As mentioned in Chapter One, turning down the house heat and creating a personal "warmth zone" in bed by sleeping under a comforter or an electric blanket reduces overall household energy consumption.

Small space heaters can serve the same purpose in a room setting. Dialing down the central heating system's thermostat and turning on a space heater in the area where heat is needed can reduce overall heating fuel usage. This works well for home offices or entertainment rooms designed for TV or movie watching. Gas and wood fireplaces and stoves, as well as portable electric heaters, can all be used in this manner.

"Ventless" gas fireplaces and kerosene space heaters should be used with caution, as both produce combustion by-products that are released into the air. These heaters are not designed to be a home's primary heat source. Read and follow all directions concerning setup and use of any space heaters.

Small Air Conditioners Can Save Money in the Summer

In the summer, installing a room air conditioner to cool a small area instead of the entire house can reduce electricity bills. Dial up the thermostat in the rest of the house to keep the central air-conditioning system from running so frequently. The power consumed by a small room air unit is much less than that used by the larger system. This strategy can also be used at night in one or two bedrooms—provided sleepers are not bothered by the noise created by a room air conditioner.

CHAPTER THREE

GET YOUR HANDS DIRTY

An investment in some maintenance time—or minor upgrading to achieve better energy efficiency of a home's existing appliances, devices, and systems—can pay money-saving dividends. Though it may require getting a bit dirty, here are some items that can usually be improved with a little effort.

THE REFRIGERATOR

Clean Refrigerator Coils

Dust on the coils under or behind a refrigerator acts as insulation and causes the compressor to work harder than it needs to in order to cool the refrigerator's contents.

Clean the refrigerator coils a couple of times a year with a vacuum cleaner and an elongated brush to help the refrigerator operate at its maximum efficiency. Move a refrigerator away from a wall so air can circulate behind it, and keep it out of direct sunlight and away from heat sources like a radiator or a range.

WATER DEVICES

Remove Sediment from a Water Heater's Tank

Periodically remove accumulated hard-water mineral sediment from a water heater's tank, and thus help it operate at optimum efficiency.

As water is heated, minerals separate from the water and fall to the bottom of the tank. The mineral deposits build up to the point that they act as insulation, isolating the water from the effect of the burner firing below (on gas and oil units) and sometimes stacking up high enough to cover the heating element on an electric water heater. The harder it is for heat to get through the sediment layer, the longer the burner has to fire or the electric elements have to run in order to heat the water. The solution is to remove the sediment layer.

It is not necessary to turn off the power source (electricity, gas, or oil) to the water heater in order to drain the sediment.

Attach a short length of standard garden hose to the drain valve at the bottom of the water heater. Place the free end of the hose into either a floor drain nearby or a large bucket, and open the valve. Water will flow from the bottom of the water heater, out the valve, and through the hose, taking sediment along with it.

Drain five gallons or so from the tank, shut off the valve, and disconnect the hose. Depending on the mineral content of the water, a water heater tank should be drained of its sediment at least twice a year and more often in hard-water areas.

Removing sediment from a water heater also helps extend its service life. There is a thin film of water trapped between the sediment and the bottom of the tank. When the burner fires, the layer of water heats to such a high temperature that the tank's glass lining deteriorates, speeding up its rusting process. Accumulated sediment is also responsible for the popping, banging, rumbling, and percolating noises often heard from a water heater as the burner fires or the elements heat up.

Beef Up Water Heater Insulation

New water heaters are built with foam insulation injected between the tank and the exterior jacket. Older units with less-efficient fiberglass insulation can benefit from a water heater "blanket," available at home centers and hardware stores. The blanket wraps the exterior in an additional layer of insulation. The more insulation on a water heater, the fewer "standby" losses will occur, the less the burner or elements will come on, and the more efficient it will be overall.

Electric water heaters can be covered top to bottom with insulation. Gas water heaters must not be covered on top or along the bottom. The top contains the flue, which can get hot enough to ignite flammable materials. The bottom must be left open so air can enter the burner assembly for proper combustion of the fuel.

The end of the pressure and temperature relief valve extension pipe (usually running down the side of the unit) on any type of water heater must be left open and exposed. This pipe has to be free of obstructions in case the valve activates to release hot water or steam. Any blockage could interfere with the release of the pressure within the tank.

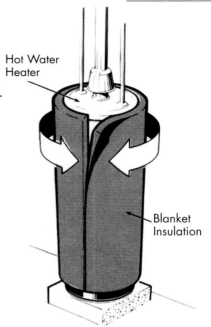

Hot Water Heater

Blanket Insulation

Insulate Water Pipes

Pipe insulation keeps heat from hot water inside the pipes where it belongs, rather than radiating out into the air. The result is that hot water reaches distant bathrooms faster than it would otherwise, reducing the volume of water that has to flow down the pipe before hot water arrives. And once hot water fills the pipe, it stays hot longer, ready for another use.

Pipe insulation also helps reduce "standby" heat losses at the water heater. Heat radiating from the water heater's tank and the pipes entering and exiting the top of the unit reduce the temperature of the water inside the tank. Eventually, the thermostat is activated and the burner fires or the electric elements switch on. The water heats up again, only to cool down gradually through the cooling effects of the tank and pipes. The endless cycle is exacerbated by heat loss through the pipes at the top of the water heater. So, although the hot water pipes are the logical ones to insulate, insulating the first five feet or so of the cold water pipe at the water heater is a good idea, too. That helps reduce the loss of heat that migrates up the pipe from the water heater tank.

Closed cell foam pipe insulation, available at plumbing supply houses and home centers, insulates well and is easy to install. Each piece is slit along its length, allowing the insulation to snap over the pipe. The foam can be cut with a knife or a pair of heavy scissors. Seams can be glued or taped for additional insulative value.

It may also be worthwhile to insulate another cold water pipe—the water service entry pipe from a municipal supply or well—though not for energy-efficiency reasons. Throughout the winter and into the spring, water coming into the house through that pipe is cold. If the air is humid enough, condensation can form on the outside of the pipe and drip down onto carpets, suspended ceiling tiles, and anything else along its path. Covering the exposed pipe with foam insulation isolates the pipe from the humid air, preventing condensation from forming.

Insulate Hot Water Boiler Pipes

Distribution pipes in water-heating systems benefit greatly from an insulation wrap. With insulation in place, hotter water gets to the radiators or convectors, increasing the efficiency of the entire system. In addition, less heat is lost to the areas through which the distribution pipes run. Closed-cell foam insulation is available in many sizes at heating supply stores.

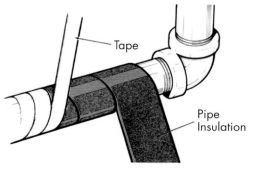

Tape

Pipe Insulation

TEMPERATURE DEVICES

Tune Up Heating, Ventilating, and Air-Conditioning (HVAC) Systems

Furnaces, boilers, and air-conditioning systems all have mechanical, moving parts in addition to electrical components. Over time these parts can go out of adjustment and need lubrication and cleaning. Like an automobile, heating and cooling equipment runs best—and at its highest efficiency—when it is "tuned up" and all the parts are working together as they were designed.

Tuning up HVAC equipment, especially the newer, more complicated systems, should be attempted only by service people who have the training and the equipment to do the work. Oil-fired systems should be serviced every year. Gas-fired furnaces and boilers and air-conditioning systems should be checked at least every two years.

Replace Furnace Filters

The filter on a forced-air furnace performs several functions. It strains bits of dust and dirt from the airstream as it passes through the furnace, improving air quality. It also protects the inside of the furnace (and air-conditioning evaporator coil, if there is one). Without a furnace filter in place, dirt would build up on the back side of the heater exchanger and inside the A/C evaporator coil. That dirt can act as insulation and interfere with the efficient transfer of heat from the furnace, or cooling from the air conditioner, to the air passing through it.

A dirty filter slows the passage of air through the furnace, robbing it of efficiency. The best way to keep a furnace operating at its maximum efficiency is to keep a clean filter inside. Filters can be purchased in bulk and replaced every 30–45 days, or they can be vacuumed at those same intervals.

Homeowners with pets may find that the furnace filter needs to be replaced or cleaned more frequently, due to pet dander, hair, and dirt brought in from outside.

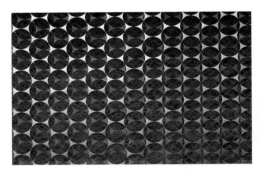

Homes equipped with a central air-conditioning system use the furnace's blower to distribute cool and dehumidified air during the summer months, necessitating filter changes or cleaning at roughly the same intervals as required during the winter.

Air-Seal Heat Ducts

Poorly installed forced-air duct systems can leak up to 25 percent of the air passing through them. The leakage might occur in basements, crawl spaces, duct chases, or attics, resulting in higher heating and air-conditioning bills, as well as a loss of comfort in the rooms where the air was intended to go.

The solution to leaky ducts is duct sealing. Regular "duct tape" is poorly suited for duct sealing. The adhesives in cloth duct tape break down in the presence of heat; eventually the tape fails and falls off the duct.

Duct-sealing mastic, available in tubs at heating supply houses, hardware stores, and home centers, is a product better suited for the application. Duct mastic is applied by manually smearing it all around every joint in the ductwork. It has the consistency of pancake batter, and once it cures, it stays on the duct and doesn't leak.

Adjust Diverter Vanes

After a sealing job is complete, diverter vanes inside the ducts (if they are installed) might have to be readjusted. Air that was supposed to go to a certain area will finally be able to do so. The result might be that a formerly cold room is suddenly the warmest one in the house.

Install Duct Insulation

After duct sealing and readjusting the duct system is complete, further energy efficiency can be achieved by wrapping any ducts passing through unheated crawl spaces or attics with insulation. Heat and cooling thrown off by the ducts in such areas is completely wasted. If that heat and cooling is retained, the furnace or air conditioner doesn't have to work overly hard to condition the house.

Duct insulation, available at home centers and heating and air-conditioning installers, is available in both wrapping and sleeve types. Sleeves are more effective because they have fewer seams, but they may require temporary disassembly of the ducts in order to slip them into place. Wrap types are good for nonstandard size ducts and areas where sliding a sleeve over a duct is not practical.

Panels of foil-faced fiberglass ductboard are also available for insulating flat, rectangular areas of ductwork.

THE HOME

Seal the Mudsill

The wooden framing in most homes rests on top of a solid concrete or concrete block foundation. In homes built before 1980, the lowest section of wood, called the "mudsill," rests directly on top of the concrete. The rough surface of the concrete does not create a good seal with the mudsill. There may be some areas where gaps allow air to enter the house.

The gaps, which collectively might add up to a hole the size of a basketball in the exterior envelope, can be sealed with

CAULK OR SPRAY FOAM— WHICH TO USE WHERE?

Two of the best products to use in dealing with gaps and holes in your home's envelope are caulk and insulating foam that comes in a spray can.

Acrylic latex caulk can be used on cracks and small openings on the exterior of a home. It can be painted and is durable enough to withstand a moderate amount of expansion and contraction due to weather extremes. It is also useful inside the home to fill gaps around window and door trim on baseboards, as well as to seal other smaller fissures.

Spray foam is available in two formulations: expanding and nonexpanding. The nonexpanding type is useful for sealing the gaps between window and door jambs in new construction and in other areas as well. Because the foam does not expand, it won't deflect the jambs inward as expanding foam tends to do.

Expanding foam is the product of choice for sealing wiring and holes that run through framing lumber. It is also used for plugging gaps between the top of a foundation wall and the start of the wood framing, around electrical boxes and vent fan housings in attics, and along the tops of room walls that intersect with the attic framing. Expanding foam can fill holes up to about 2 inches in diameter.

either caulk or cans of spray foam. The procedure can be done either on the inside or outside of the house (depending on which allows the best access). It requires brushing away dirt and cobwebs from the concrete and wood so the caulk or foam will stick to both surfaces.

Aim the caulk tube's tip or spray foam applicator tube at the gaps and gun them full of caulk or foam. Neatness is not important; thoroughness is.

In newer homes, any space between the mudsill and the top of the foundation wall is filled with a length of thin, compressible foam material. The foam creates an airtight seal that usually does not need remedial caulking or foaming. Occasionally, however, the foam sealer is not correctly placed. Also, the top of the foundation wall might be too uneven for the foam to fill the gap, or it might stop short of the corners. A shot of caulk or foam quickly remedies these problems.

Caulk Air-Conditioning Refrigerant Line Holes

HVAC system installers need to bore a sizable hole through the exterior wall of the house in order to pass refrigerant lines through. Most take time to caulk the hole around the lines, but the caulk fails over time, often leaving a gap where air (and insects) can infiltrate the house. A few minutes spent with a caulk gun will close the gap and eliminate that source of air leakage.

Caulk Doors, Windows, and Other Openings

Use paintable latex caulk to close off cracks or holes around doors and windows to stop air infiltration and keep water out of the building's structure. Excluding water prevents wood rot and extends the service life of an exterior paint job.

Air can also enter a house through cracks in the siding and through other openings like kitchen and bathroom vent fan louvers, dryer vents, electrical and gas service wires, and pipes, along the underside of the lowest course of siding, and through other holes. Filling or sealing any of these holes and gaps reduces air infiltration and exfiltration and increases the home's overall energy efficiency.

Weather-strip Exterior Doors

Proper sealing of doors in their openings plays a major part in weatherizing the outside of a house. The most effective types of easily applied door weather stripping contain a vinyl bulb or padded strip set into the edge of a conventional wood doorstop. The wood part is nailed to the doorjamb and is flexible enough to conform even to a warped wooden door. The vinyl bulb or strip seals out air movement but is compressible enough that the door's function is not affected.

Other types of weather stripping, more difficult and time-consuming to install, include thin bronze or brass strips that are nailed inside the jamb where the door closes. When the door closes, it strikes the metal strip, bending it a bit and ensuring tight contact with the door edge. This type of weather stripping lasts for years and is an effective draft stopper.

Some contractors are equipped to install a type of vinyl bulb weather stripping that is cut into the door frame with a special tool. The tool resembles a router and cuts a small groove into the intersection of the doorstop and the jamb. A barbed fin on vinyl bulb weather strip is pressed into the groove; friction keeps it there. This type of weather stripping is very effective if installed properly. The hard part is finding someone who has the equipment and know-how to install it.

Repair or Upgrade Storm Doors

Storm doors add draft-stopping ability, insulation, and protection to a home's entry doors. Aluminum storm doors have frames that screw to the outside of the door casing. There might be gaps between the frame and the casing, and those can be filled with caulk.

Another area of potential air infiltration is the door bottom. Most storm doors have an adjustable door bottom that can slide up or down once the screws holding it in place are loosened. The adjustability allows the door bottom to fit snugly against the door's threshold.

The vinyl strip that seals the bottom of a storm door to the edge of the threshold can tear or wear out over time. Similarly, the weather stripping that is attached to the frame and contacts the face of the door as it closes must be in good condition for the storm door to function as it was designed. Generic replacements are available, but original material from the manufacturer usually fits best.

Repair or Upgrade Storm Windows

Storm windows can play a key role in an energy saving plan. They act as a wind buffer, and the air trapped between the storms and the prime windows acts as insulation. Storm windows also protect the prime windows from the weather, which can extend the time between paint jobs required inside the house.

Older homes are often equipped with heavy wooden storm windows that need to be put up in the fall and taken down in the spring, when they are usually replaced with wooden-framed screens. Newer options, and a worthy upgrade to wooden storm windows, include permanently installed aluminum or vinyl storms, which self-store the window glazing and screens. Instead of lugging large storm windows up and down a ladder twice a year, the glazing or screen portions slide up or down into position, reconfiguring the storm window depending on the season.

Many homeowners with aluminum or vinyl storms choose to remove the lightweight screen portion during the winter, preferring to look only through window glass instead of screening. Not only is the window glass more aesthetically pleasing, sunlight can also shine more directly into the house without a screen in place, allowing greater solar heating.

Another advantage to storm windows is that the extra layer of glazing cuts down on neighborhood and traffic noise. Storms also keep out dust and dirt that otherwise might filter into the home through leaky prime windows.

Energy Saving Landscaping

The configuration of the landscape outside a house can help save energy inside. Trees planted along the side of a property can blunt the force of the prevailing wind, as can a fence or shrubbery. Blocking the wind reduces the amount of heat swept off that side of the house.

Trees also play a big part in reducing cooling expenses in the summer. Shade from a large tree reduces the temperature of the air surrounding a house by an average of ten degrees, and it can block sunlight from penetrating where it is not wanted. The cooler the air outside the house, the less temperature differential the A/C system has to maintain with the inside air.

Deciduous trees are especially valuable for energy saving landscape schemes. They block the sun's unwanted rays during the summer, then drop their leaves and allow sunlight into the house during the winter.

Caulk Doors, Windows, and Other Areas Inside the House

Once the exterior of the home is sealed as well as possible, it is valuable to do the same to the inside. Gaps are often left between baseboards and hard floors, such as tile, hardwood, or laminate flooring. Fill these areas with latex caulk to prevent air from entering the home at foot level.

Seasonal wood movement can create cracks around window and door casings, and don't forget to look at their tops. It's not unusual to find large gaps between the casing and drywall or plaster. Any fissures found in these areas should be caulked.

Infiltration and exfiltration don't only occur between the indoors and outside. Air can also move within a house from the basement or the interior rooms up into the attic and beyond. So it's also beneficial to caulk around all the interior doors and around as much of the interior baseboard as possible.

The framing around laundry chutes, as well as pipe and wire chases from the basement to the upper floors, deserve caulking or spray foam attention too.

Understanding the "Stack Effect"

Warm air rises. It is the reason hot air rises up a fireplace flue. What isn't commonly known is that rising warm air creates pressure at the top of whatever is containing it. In a household situation, the top-floor ceiling acts as a containment barrier to rising warm air. As such, any small hole or gap in that area is subject to pressurized warm air trying to escape.

Warm air loss due to the stack effect has another consequence. As air exits through the top-floor ceiling or other holes, it creates slight negative pressure inside the house. The exiting air has to be replaced, and that replacement air comes from outside the house: cold, dry air. It infiltrates through any convenient hole it can find. The incoming air has to be heated, and that's when the furnace or boiler comes on.

The stack effect is why it is extremely important to seal any holes or gaps in the attic floor and top floor ceiling.

Upgrade Pull-Down Attic Stairways

A pull-down attic stairway can represent the largest hole in a home's ceiling—a hole through which a tremendous amount of air can flow in both winter and summer. Energy experts estimate that the gap around a typical pull-down stairway system can amount to 40 square inches.

The underside of many pull-down attic stair units is made of ¼-inch plywood that warps away from its sealing surfaces shortly after installation. Springs that hold the stairway in place lose their resilience, allowing the unit to sag down from the opening and open gaps between the plywood and the jamb. Even in the best of circumstances the entirety of the stair system is uninsulated. It's a worst-case scenario in terms of air sealing and energy efficiency.

To help reduce air leakage, add compressible self-stick foam tape along the upper edges of the plywood door, as well as to the eyehooks or another type of latching device to the door to jam it tight against the foam weather stripping when it's not in use.

A more comprehensive solution is to install a "kit" that insulates and air-seals the door at the same time. "Attic tents" consist of a clothlike material that is caulked and stapled to the framing around the stairway opening in the attic. A zipper in the upper part of the tent can be opened for access and closed for air sealing after use. The stairway opens and closes normally underneath the tent fabric. An attic tent, however, provides only a small measure of insulative value compared to the insulation that should be on the rest of the attic floor.

Another available kit is a thick, rigid foam box that surrounds the stairway opening in the attic. A removable cover in the attic lifts off when access to the attic is desired. Sealing strips along the bottom of the box contact the framing around the stairway or the attic floor. By using rigid foam board and other easily obtainable materials, a homeowner can construct a similar box.

Insulate and Air-Seal the Attic Hatch

The way attic access scuttleholes are usually constructed makes them vulnerable to air leakage.

Many consist of thin, uninsulated pieces of plywood that have warped and cannot seal airtight to their frames. Pressurized warm air lying along the ceiling waits to escape through the gaps between the hatch and frame.

A more energy-efficient attic hatch can be made out of flat ¾-inch plywood with several inches of rigid foam board glued to the back. Self-stick compressible foam tape can be applied to the top of the frame where the hatch door rests. The hatch can be fitted with eyehooks that snug it down against the foam, assuring the foam's compression and a more airtight seal.

Air-Seal the Attic Floor

Most attics have at least some insulation in them, and insulation, of course, helps stop heat loss. It doesn't stop airflow, however, and that's a problem.

The insulation lying on attic floors often conceals cracks, gaps, and holes through which pressurized air from the house below is driven into the attic. The fissures take many forms: holes that were drilled into the wood framing for wiring; electrical boxes for lighting fixtures; areas where the tops of partition walls in the room below intersect with the attic-floor framing; bulkheads over kitchen and bathroom cabinets; exhaust vent fans; and fireplace and heating equipment chimneys and flues. Every opening represents an opportunity for warm air to escape the rooms below.

The materials used for sealing most attic floor penetrations are caulk and spray foam. The application

SHOULD A CEILING FAN BLOW DOWN OR UP?

There is a switch on the side of most ceiling fans that controls the direction of the blade rotation. In the summer it's best if the blades blow air downward onto the occupants of the room. That provides a cooling, wind-chill effect as air blows over the skin.

In the winter, however, the downward push of air can make the room feel drafty and cooler than it really is. Thus that's the time of year to switch the blade rotation so the fan pulls air upward. That moves stratified warm air off the ceiling and down along the walls, creating a more even mix of air in the room.

does not have to be neat, but it must be thorough. Any gap left unfilled will leak air. Once the foam or caulk has been applied, insulation can be pushed back into place over the remediated area.

In an attic filled with unfaced fiberglass insulation, spots where air is leaking show up as gray or black smudges or staining in the fiberglass. The discolored spots are dirt that was borne on the air leaking from below, filtered out by the fiberglass. Under the stains will be an opening into the room below, maybe an electrical box or wire chase. Attics insulated with cellulose fiber don't show air-leak smudges. The material is as dark as most airborne dirt, and it doesn't act as a filter.

Examine rooms below before entering the attic. Take note of where light fixtures and interior walls are located.

Once a hole is located, use a brush to sweep the insulation back. Then squirt caulk or spray foam to seal the hole or gap. After replacing the insulation, move on to the next spot. Be especially aware that many interior walls have wires running up into the attic. Foam around the wires to fill the holes in the framing.

Electrical boxes should have the power switched off before working around them. Caulk around the box where it penetrates the drywall or plaster and around the wires that run into the box. Vent fan housings are sealed in a similar manner.

Chimneys require a different approach. Fire and building codes mandate at least a two-inch gap between any flammable material (usually wood framing) and the masonry or metal. Sheet metal nailed to the framing and pushed against the chimney can bridge the gap. Fire resistant caulk can seal up any remaining opening.

Seal Windows Temporarily for the Winter

The amount of cold air leaking through windows during the winter often dismays owners of older homes that still have their original windows. Using a caulk gun and "weather stripping caulk sealant" to temporarily seal up the cracks can stop air infiltration between the window and window frame.

Weather stripping sealant is caulk that is sticky enough to remain in place but can be peeled off when it is no longer needed. It is available inexpensively in regular caulk tubes and comes in a clear color. Nearly invisible, it removes easily without damaging either paint or clear finishes.

Weatherize the Shared Garage/House Wall

Homes with attached garages often have "interface" problems that can lead to the waste of heat and cooling. Because the garage is attached to the house, in many cases the effort that goes into sealing the outside of the house against the weather is not extended to the garage. But in the winter the garage can become just as cold as the outdoor air—and in the summer, even hotter than it is outside.

Holes in garage walls, intentional or accidental, often allow air movement between the two areas. Not only are these potential pathways for heated or cooled air to escape or infiltrate, but they also can present several dangers.

Filling Gaps in the Garage/House Wall Saves Energy, Reduces Hazards

The solution to the dangers of a compromised garage/house wall is to make every effort to seal areas where air might be able to pass between the house and garage. Prime trouble spots are the bottom of the wall inside the garage and the bottom of the doorway into the house.

There is a seam between the framing and concrete where the bottom of the wall meets the concrete foundation. It is similar to the one around the perimeter of the rest of the house, and it should be dealt with in the same manner. This location sometimes lacks a layer of compressible foam between the two materials, foam that would provide an airtight seal. Caulk or spray foam applied either inside the basement (as previously described in the section on sealing this seam) or in the garage can effectively seal the gap.

It is also worth using caulk or foam to seal the bottom edges of the drywall to the concrete. In negative pressure situations, air can be drawn into this crack or into the stud cavities inside the wall. It can then enter the house via an electrical receptacle on the other side of the wall inside the house. Adding gaskets to receptacles on both sides of the wall also helps in keeping contaminated garage air out of the house.

The door into the house from the garage is often a leak point as well. Caulking around all the trim and an examination of the door's weather stripping to ensure it is intact will help block off this potential air passageway. The door bottom must contact the threshold in the way it was designed to do in order to keep air out. Frequently used doors like the one from the garage into the house might need repair or replacement of the weather stripping more frequently than other entry doors.

CHAPTER FOUR

MAKE IMPROVEMENTS AROUND THE HOUSE

Putting a significant amount of money toward purchasing or upgrading something in order to reduce energy consumption and save money on utility bills is a wise investment and makes good sense. In fact, the money invested can actually pay a better return than many traditional "investment" options, such as stocks and bonds.

Investing in the latest, most technologically advanced mechanical equipment and appliances means the benefits begin immediately and keep paying off every day from that point forward. And all the "returns" are tax-free!

PRIORITIZING

Implement Upgrades in the Correct Order for the Best Results

What is the best place to start when weatherizing a house? Air sealing is usually the first priority. Sealing as many of the gaps and holes as possible in the attic ceiling and on the home's exterior reduces the amount of air that escapes the house and leaks into the attic and outdoors. After air sealing is complete, attic insulation can be blown or laid on top of the air-sealed attic floor.

If replacing windows and heating or air-conditioning systems, have the windows replaced first. When a contractor sizes the equipment for the expected heating and cooling load of the house, he or she will consider the completed energy upgrades. If there are new windows in place and thick insulation in the attic, plus a good amount of air sealing done, the result is that cooling and heating loads will be reduced. The house may be able to get by with smaller (and less expensive) heating and cooling equipment.

ENERGY STAR

Choosing Energy Star Appliances

In 1992, the federal government launched an energy-efficiency rating program called "Energy Star." The

LEARN MORE AT energystar.gov

Environmental Protection Agency (EPA) and the Department of Energy (DOE) administer Energy Star. The Energy Star Web site at www.energystar.gov provides appliance ratings and tips on improving the energy performance in homes and businesses.

The appliance-labeling program, perhaps the most visible of Energy Star's endeavors, rates major appliances and provides information that allows consumers to make energy-wise choices about these products.

How Much Can New Appliances Save?

Energy Star-qualified appliances exceed federal energy-efficiency standards by 10 to 50 percent. As an example, Energy Star-rated refrigerators use better-quality insulation, more efficient compressors, and more sophisticated temperature-control mechanisms, delivering 15 percent better energy savings than other models that only meet the current government standards.

Because a refrigerator typically uses the most energy of any appliance in a household, these energy improvements can make a noticeable difference in energy and money saved. Energy Star-rated freezers use comparable technical improvements to yield at least a 10-percent premium on energy savings.

Similar numbers show up in ratings for dishwashers, clothes washers, dehumidifiers, ceiling fans, heating and cooling units, and other equipment. And while Energy Star-rated appliances and electronic devices usually bear a higher price tag than models without the Energy Star certification, the extra cost is more than made up in savings over the lifetime of the product.

Energy Star-rated appliances, such as dishwashers and clothes washers, make the most sense in homes where they are frequently used. Larger homes, or ones that are located in severe climate areas like the north or the south, can save the most by using Energy Star-rated heating and cooling equipment.

APPLIANCES

Get Rid of That Old Refrigerator or Freezer

"Auxiliary" refrigerators or freezers in garages or basements are energy hogs. Usually less efficient than newer models, older models might cost up to 30 dollars a month just to keep beverages cold. A hot garage environment makes the inefficient compressor work even harder to achieve cooling.

Invest in a New Refrigerator

Refrigerators at least ten years old require nearly twice the energy to run as do new models with better insulation and more efficient compressors. Replacing a refrigerator of that vintage with a new one could reduce an electricity bill by five dollars or more every month: 60 dollars a year. If the new refrigerator costs $600, the "yield" would be 10 percent return on investment—much more than banks are paying on savings accounts, checking accounts, or certificates of deposit. An extra bonus is that money "earned" on energy savings isn't subject to state or federal income tax.

Use the Range Hood to Save Energy

Range hoods that vent outdoors to remove cooking odors, humidity, heat, and combustion by-products from gas ranges and ovens are superior to those that only recirculate

REFRIGERATOR WARS

There is now a way to find out how much that old refrigerator or freezer sitting in your garage or basement costs to run every year. *Home Energy Magazine* has mounted an online searchable database (approximately 85,000 refrigerators and freezers), along with their energy ratings at http://www.homeenergy.org/consumerinfo/refrigeration2/refmods.html.

To get the lowdown on your refrigerator, you'll need its make and model number—for instance, Amana, TJ18KW. This information can usually be found on a label plate somewhere inside the food compartment or on the front edge of the refrigerator's frame.

After entering the numbers into the site's search engine, the energy ratings will appear on your computer screen. The database lists the date of manufacture, size of the unit, the amount of energy it consumed when it was new, and how much energy it uses at its current age.

For the Amana above, the 17.78-cubic-foot top-freezer model built in 1988 used 856 kilowatt-hours of electricity per year when it was new. In 2005, that amount climbed to 1,112 kilowatt-hours. At a rate of 10 cents per kilowatt-hour the refrigerator costs $111.20 a year to operate. Since your electrical rate per kilowatt-hour may differ, find the charge on your utility bill.

By comparison, a new 18.4-cubic-foot top-freezer Amana uses only 409 kilowatt-hours of electricity a year—$40.90, an annual savings of $70.30.

air. Outdoor-venting hoods remove heat from the house and are worth upgrading from a recirculating model.

Purchase a New, Front-Loading Clothes Washer

Front-loading machines use only one third to one half the water per load required by conventional top loaders. Because some wash water may need to be heated, reducing the amount used means the water heater doesn't have to fire as long, resulting in energy savings—with water savings as a bonus.

These machines clean clothes by dropping them through and dipping them into water repeatedly during the wash cycle instead of swishing them back and forth, as is the norm in top-loading washers. The drum spins on a horizontal axis rather than a vertical one. Tests indicate that this type of washing action cleans clothes more thoroughly, yet gently. Because front loaders use less water, they need less soap and bleach to clean clothes. Many, however, require the use of special low-sudsing detergents in order to work properly.

Front loaders also use high-speed rinse and water-extraction cycles. Some can spin the drum at 1,400 rpm, which yields more thorough removal of water and soap residue than top loaders. Because higher spin speeds remove more water, clothing needs less time to dry, which yields savings. Shortened drying times also mean clothing items have less contact with each other in the high-heat dryer environment, helping the fabric last longer.

Some new front loaders include a heating element that can be activated much like the one in a dishwasher to heat water in the machine higher than the temperature the household water heater produces. This feature can be used for special purposes, for instance to sanitize baby wear or to wash sheets and pillowcases during cold and flu season.

Front-loading washing machines and matching dryers can be stacked atop one another, saving valuable floor space; a laundry pair might be able to fit into an area where a conventional side-by-side setup couldn't go.

Buy a New Top Loading Washing Machine

To keep pace with the interest in water and energy-saving front loaders, manufacturers of top-loading machines now offer models with competing features. Some new machines on the market have no central agitator. Others offer high-speed water-extraction spin cycles. Most use less water than previous designs and consequently require less soap and bleach. Some, however, need low-suds detergent to operate optimally.

WATER HEATERS

Weigh the Benefits and Potential Drawbacks of Tankless Water Heaters

Tankless water heaters contain a burner or electrical heating element that heats water flowing through a coil in the unit. Open a hot-water tap and the burner or heating element comes on; shut the tap and the burner or element shuts off, and water heating ceases.

Tankless water heaters are energy-efficient in large part because they suffer none of the "standby" heat loss inherent in standard "storage" tank type water heaters. During the time periods between uses, heat from a 40- or 50-gallon conventional water heater tank is eventually transferred to the surrounding air, and the burner or heating element must activate in order to keep the volume of water in the tank hot. The standby heat loss also contributes to the cooling load of an air-conditioning system during the summer.

Because there is no storage tank and large volume of water to keep hot, tankless water heaters do not undergo standby losses. Moreover, compared to storage type units, burners in tankless units are more efficient at transferring heat to the water flowing through the coil.

Another advantage to using a tankless water heater, though it has nothing to do with energy savings or efficiency, is that the household never runs out of hot water. There is never a wait for water in a tank to heat up sufficiently to make it tolerable for use.

Higher end tankless heaters contain variable-capacity burners that automatically adjust their firing to the volume and temperature of the water passing through the heat exchanger, resulting in more efficient heating and more precise output temperature. Ignition is supplied by a sparking device, eliminating energy loss from a standing pilot light.

Hung on a wall, tankless units don't take up any floor space. Because they are small, they may be located near a point of use, cutting down on the plumbing pipe needed for installation—and the wait for hot water, for instance, to a bathroom distant from the basement. The service life of the unit should be 20 years or more, compared to 8–15 years for a storage type tank water heater.

The Downside of Tankless Water Heaters

Looking into installing a tankless water heater will likely bring up issues about the expense of installation, gas piping, venting, and electricity. Gas fired models (which have the highest capacity, and thus are the most popular type) require a flue to vent combustion by-products created by the burner's firing. Because burners on tankless water heaters demand a high volume of gas, they require a larger-than-normal flue to safely vent the combustion gases.

Some tankless units can vent out a sidewall, requiring cutting a hole somewhere in the perimeter of the house. Conventionally vented models aren't a simple swap out for a storage-type water heater. Problems may crop up with accommodating a larger vent in an existing installation.

Because of a tankless water heater's outsized burner capacity, gas piping might have to be replaced with a larger size in order to deliver the amount of gas necessary for the water heater to operate correctly. And most tankless water heaters require electricity to operate, meaning a new receptacle might have to be added if one is not already within six feet of the planned installation.

Dependence on electricity means the water heater won't heat water during power outages, though some of the newest models on the market are designed to operate independent of outside power.

The heat exchanger inside a tankless water heater requires periodic descaling in hard-water areas, using a mild acid liquid.

The burner in a tankless water heater will come on only when a certain volume of water is used, usually around a half gallon a minute. And water might take an additional 5–15 seconds to heat as it goes through the heat exchanger, so the wait for hot water is usually extended. Recently, "hybrid" water heaters, consisting of a small storage tank combined with a tankless burner, have come onto the market to address these issues.

The initial cost of a tankless water heater is several times that of a storage-type water heater. Additional money is required for installation expenses. But in homes where a considerable amount of hot water is used and the occupants can live with some of a tankless water heater's quirks, investing in one can result in energy savings over its lifetime.

Adequate Sizing of Tankless Water Heaters Is Critical

Tankless water heaters are rated by their ability to raise the temperature of the water coming into the unit at a certain flow rate. If it isn't sized properly, the water heater won't be capable of delivering enough water to serve several uses at the same time. In northern climates, water may come into a home through underground piping at 38 degrees. It takes a lot of energy to heat water that cold to a usable 120 degrees.

To ensure that the water is being heated to the correct temperature, an undersized tankless water heater might have to slow the flow rate through the heat exchanger. This can result in a lower-than-expected volume of water at the hot-water tap or shower.

Similarly, if two people in the house want to use hot water at the same time, they might have to share the hot water coming out of the water heater, and neither is likely to be satisfied with how much they are getting. The key to avoiding these problems is to purchase a tankless water heater with enough capacity to deal with any circumstance. The other option is to accept and work around some of the limitations of a smaller model.

HEATING AND COOLING SYSTEMS

Replace an Inefficient Furnace

From the 1950s through the early 1980s, most furnaces had efficiency ratings of about 65 percent. That meant approximately 35 percent of the heat the furnace produced was lost up the fluepipe. Over the last couple of decades the ratings of all furnaces have risen to the point that some can boast as much as 95 percent efficiency.

Currently, national standards require that furnaces yield a minimum of 78-percent efficiency, so it is possible to purchase one with a rating between 78 percent and 95 percent. Furnaces at opposite ends of the spectrum differ markedly in how they operate. It is important to know the difference between how each functions before talking with a contractor about possibly replacing an outdated or defective unit.

High- Versus Standard-Efficiency Furnaces

All forced-air furnaces need to mix air with the fuel they burn to combust properly. How a furnace gets that air is an important dividing line between lower- and high-efficiency furnaces. Lower-efficiency furnaces draw "combustion air" from the room in which they are installed; high-efficiency furnaces draw it directly from outside the house.

Whenever the burner on a standard-efficiency furnace starts up, it draws air into the combustion chamber. That air is burned along with the fuel and sent up the fluepipe. The air comes from within the house, and therefore has been previously heated by the furnace. As the furnace draws in air to burn, new air has to come from somewhere to replace that which is being burned up and vented outside. The combustion air is drawn into the house through windows, doors, and cracks or gaps in the exterior walls. This creates dry conditions, drafts, and inefficiency, because the furnace has to heat the incoming cold air.

High-efficiency, or "sealed-combustion," furnaces draw combustion air from outside the house via a PVC plastic intake pipe. Since the air is coming directly into the firebox from outside, room air is not being burned up and vented out the flue. Because there is no demand for additional air drawn from within the house, there is no continual influx of cold, dry air from outside. The result is much greater efficiency, fewer drafts, not as many problems with dry air, and a warmer, more comfortable house.

Upgrade to a Two-Speed or Variable-Speed Furnace

While 95-percent-efficiency furnaces offer homeowners the greatest benefit in terms of energy savings, lower rated units have also evolved to provide better comfort and efficiency. One feature showing up on many new sub-90-percent furnaces are two-stage or variable-speed burners.

Older furnaces had only one firing capacity; the burner was either on or it was off. On a chilly-but-not-cold day, that meant the furnace might come on for only a few minutes and then shut off again, having quickly raised the indoor temperature. Running a furnace that way is inefficient. It can be compared to starting a car to drive only a few blocks, then shutting it off only to turn it on again to drive a few more blocks. Cars and furnaces are both more efficient when they can run at their optimum operating temperatures.

Two-stage and variable-speed furnaces use sensors to control the flow rate of the fuel through the burner. On chilly-but-not-cold days, the furnace runs at the low setting but for a longer period of time. This allows it to operate at the most efficient temperature and without the many stops and starts that create inefficient burning. On cold days, it burns at full capacity to accommodate the greater demand for heat. Most two-stage and variable-speed furnaces run at low settings approximately 90 percent of the time.

In addition to saving money, running the burner and blower longer at low settings distributes air in rooms more evenly and pulls more air through the furnace filter, which results in cleaner air.

New furnaces are quieter as well as more efficient. Virtually any new model will be quieter than one ten years old or older. The interior of the metal cabinet is lined with sound-absorbing material, and blower-fan blades are engineered and balanced to reduce noise. Two-stage and variable-speed furnaces are especially quiet. A burner firing at low capacity produces less noise than one firing at full throttle, and the blower-fan speed can be reduced to integrate with the lower heat output. The combination hushes the sound of the air rushing from the heat registers.

Upgrade to a More Efficient Boiler

Everything said about new furnaces can be applied to new gas- and oil-fired boilers. They're smaller, quieter, and more efficient (and have efficiency ratings similar to those on furnaces). They also have more sophisticated controls, and some even have variable-capacity burners.

High-end boilers also offer sealed combustion, which eliminates the consumption of house air burned up and vented outside when the burner fires. Sensors mounted outside the house can record the temperature and adjust the boiler's water temperature output to the conditions outdoors. Features like these make boiler installation more expensive and the systems more complex but also much more energy-efficient than previous models.

Deciding to Replace a Furnace or Boiler

Because every house and every situation is different, it is impossible to say whether or not a replacement furnace or boiler makes good economic sense. But for those living in a large house in a cold climate and paying elevated prices for gas or oil, the scale tips in favor of the higher-efficiency models.

For a small house or a temperate climate, paying a premium for a super high-efficiency furnace can extend the "payback" time and may make less sense from a strict economic standpoint. In that case a less expensive two-stage or variable-speed furnace, or a simpler boiler, might be the better value. A quality HVAC installer will take time to analyze each specific situation and recommend the best solution for every need and budget.

Check into whether the local utility company or state energy office offers a rebate toward higher-efficiency heating and cooling equipment. Some do, and the amount tendered can at times pay the difference between a lower- and a higher-efficiency model.

Upgrading a Central Air-Conditioning System

Air-conditioning compressors are rated by their seasonal energy efficiency ratio (SEER). Higher numbers mean better efficiency. Like replacing a furnace, homeowners with larger homes and more severe cooling needs (in hotter climates) benefit the most by replacing older A/C compressors with the most efficient new models.

Air-conditioning systems degrade over time. Many A/C systems ten years old and older may be operating at only 6–9 SEER. The highest-efficiency central A/C units on the market today are rated at about 17–18 SEER. Upgrading your A/C system can save a substantial amount of energy and money.

Another advantage of new A/C units is that they run more quietly than previous models, an important factor for those who spend time outdoors around the house or if neighbors are close by. It's also a benefit if bedrooms are located close to where the outdoor compressor is situated.

Deciding on Variable-Speed and Two-Stage Compressors

As A/C units evolve and become more efficient, engineers devise ways of making them work harder to achieve better comfort. A recent innovation is to equip air conditioners with two-stage compressors, which operate somewhat similarly to a two-stage furnace. On warm-but-not-hot days the compressor runs using only the lower stage.

The lower stage provides adequate cooling, but the compressor runs more quietly and for a longer period of time, which gives the system more of an opportunity to remove moisture from the air. The lower the humidity indoors, the higher it is possible to set the thermostat and still provide comfortable cooling, which results in energy savings.

Variable-speed blowers alter the speed of the blower motor to most efficiently match the output of the air conditioner's compressor and condenser. The outcome is better usage of the available amount of cooling, less electricity consumption, and lower energy bills.

Proper Installation Is Important

Like a heating system, a cooling system has to be installed correctly and sized accurately in order to work well and maintain the efficiency for which it was designed.

Installers use computer software to incorporate such information as window size and placement, insulation found in attics and sidewalls, square footage, orientation and geographical location of the house, and other factors into their sizing calculations. This enables precise determinations as to which air conditioner suits a particular house.

WINDOWS

Replace or upgrade windows for better air sealing, insulation, and energy savings

Virtually any new window purchased these days will have at least two panes of glass making up the glazing. Only those designed for use in unheated areas like garages are likely to have a single pane. Two-pane, or insulated, glass has proven its worth over the decades. Sandwiching air between two separated, sealed panes substantially increases the insulative value of the glazing. In recent years, manufacturers have also improved glazing performance by sealing gases like argon and krypton, which have more density and better insulative qualities than plain air, inside that space.

The glass in the assembly can also be coated with nearly invisible films, like Low-e metallic oxides, that can be manipulated to impart various properties to the window, such as better heat retention or solar heat reduction. The sash that holds the glazing is important to the overall thermal performance of the window. Materials that offer low heat conductance, like wood, hollow or insulation-filled vinyl, or fiberglass, help reduce the transference of cold inside and heat outside.

Better windows mean greater comfort, convenience, and energy efficiency

INSTALL WINDOW SHADES FOR ENERGY SAVINGS

Adding or upgrading window drapes or shades can cut heat and cooling losses significantly. In addition, they provide privacy, solar heat and light control, and a reduction of sound transmission from outside the house. Simple vinyl, wood, or metal slatted window blinds don't add much insulative value.

The heavier and more solid the shade, the better the energy conservation qualities. Lining any type of shade increases its thickness and insulative effectiveness. "Cellular" or "honeycomb" shades unfold to create air pockets between layers of the material, and some even pack the "cells" with cotton batt-type insulation.

Sealing the sides and bottom of the shade or drape to the window trim and sill makes the installation even more effective. Some shade systems come with magnetic strips that mount on the trim and have corresponding metal material sewn into the shade. As the shades come down or unfold, the strip and trim form a relatively airtight seal.

Energy-efficient window technology has also increased the comfort factor. Sitting next to a single-pane window in the winter can feel cold, even when the house itself is sufficiently warm. Body heat is radiated out the window. But energy-efficient glazing keeps the inside pane of glass warmer. That reflects body heat back inside, increasing comfort and saving energy.

Homeowners who are either tired of or not capable of climbing ladders to clean windows outside the house will appreciate the tilt-in sash feature on most new windows. With just a flick of a finger, the sash tilts inward for access to the exterior glass for cleaning.

Another important improvement to modern windows is the increase in the performance of weather stripping that stops air from infiltrating. Leakiness adds up to wasted energy. Properly installed new windows won't leak air and will save energy as a result.

Installing new windows in an existing home can make the house "live larger." If the old windows are so leaky and inefficient that the cold prevents sitting beside them in the winter, the home's occupants may feel confined to a smaller area of the house. The same might be said of a window's inability to block out sun or heat in southern climates. New windows might allow sitting nearer the exterior walls of the house in greater comfort—in effect, increasing its square footage. Beyond energy savings, upgraded windows make a house feel cozier, quieter, warmer, and more secure.

Good Installation Helps with Performance

Even good windows will not live up to their billing if they are installed improperly. That's why selecting an experienced, conscientious installer is important to maximize both the energy efficiency and satisfaction with the window purchase. A poor installation can result in water leaks, dysfunctional opening and closing, poor energy performance, and air leakage. This is particularly true when it comes to replacement windows, where old materials have to be incorporated into the new installation.

Old Windows—Worth Keeping and Upgrading?

Despite all the advantages of new windows, economic or historical concerns may be a factor in considering window upgrading. While it is true that no original single-pane glass window can match the thermal performance of a new window, it's surprising how close it can come—albeit with a lot of work.

In a house with historical features, it is worth considering restoring rather than replacing the original windows. There are situations when even the best new windows look out of place, and one of those is in a house that was designed and built with architecturally significant windows. While not impossible to duplicate today, such windows may be prohibitively expensive to reproduce. The solution is to make the existing windows as energy-efficient as possible.

Old windows usually require at least scraping and painting, and perhaps glazing compound replacement, as well as repair to broken sash cords or chains just to get them working again. If they are in poor condition, some might require regluing the joints, epoxy or wood repairs to the sash, and maybe replacement of cracked or broken panes.

From there, adding weather stripping around the perimeter of the window sash and along the meeting rail between double-hung windows can upgrade the thermal performance. Installing raft-blocking devices that plug the cord or chain holes can reduce the amount of air infiltration from those portals. To achieve even better efficiency, adding storm windows either outside the house or to the interior will help reduce energy losses.

If every advantage is taken, if all weather stripping is installed properly, and if storm windows are added to the outside, it is possible to achieve near-new window performance with old windows. Window restoration is a good job for those handy enough to do the repairs or with the means to hire professionals. Older windows can last for 100 years or more if maintained attentively.

CHAPTER FIVE

CONSIDER WHOLE-HOUSE ISSUES

Houses are made up of many different components that work together as a system. If one part is changed, the other parts are affected. Making a house more airtight and energy efficient alters the way it functions.

VENTILATION

Potential Hazards of Weatherizing a House

A previously unweatherized house typically has a leaky shell. Air from outside is free to infiltrate and exfiltrate through various uncaulked and unfilled cracks, gaps, and holes in the exterior. After stopping up those leaks by replacing old windows and by caulking, many of the pathways through which air formerly entered the house are eliminated.

From the standpoint of saving energy this is a good thing. The less air that leaves the house the less heating and cooling are needed to replace it. But is there such a thing as a house that is too airtight? The answer is that it isn't possible to make a house too airtight. It is possible, however, to make a house poorly ventilated. So where is the dividing line?

Prevent Carbon Monoxide Problems

Fuel-burning systems in a house, such as furnaces, boilers, water heaters, fireplaces, and gas clothes dryers, require a reliable influx of air to operate properly. If a house is made relatively airtight AND not enough combustion air is provided for these fuel-burners, problems can result.

When the burner on a fuel-burning appliance fires up, it draws air into a combustion chamber. The air mixes with the fuel, the mixture is burned up, and the exhaust gases are vented outside. This "combustion air" has to come from somewhere. The air that is used and then expelled has to be replaced or "made up" somehow.

In poorly weatherized houses, "makeup air" enters through the variety of gaps in the building's exterior shell. They are the paths of least resistance. If a home's exterior is air-sealed and provisions are not made to provide the fuel-

CARBON MONOXIDE DANGER

Combustion by-products produced by fuel-burning appliances contain carbon monoxide gas, a poison that is taken up by the body's red blood cells in place of oxygen. According to the Consumer Product Safety Commission (CPSC), approximately 125 people in the United States die every year from carbon-monoxide poisoning. Some of those deaths are attributed to backdrafting conditions and other venting problems from fuel-burning devices.

Backdrafting can also occur when exterior-vented fan devices, such as a kitchen range hood or bathroom ventilation fan, operate. Anything that pushes air out of the house reduces the air pressure inside, and makeup air has to come from somewhere in order to replace the air that is lost. The more airtight the house, the greater the potential for backdrafting.

The solution to backdrafting is to provide enough makeup air for fuel-burning equipment to operate correctly. Building codes require a makeup air inlet to be piped into the mechanical room in all new homes. Older homes, however, often lack such a pipe. Therefore, consultation with a furnace or boiler service person is recommended before any tightening of a home's shell is undertaken. If a home doesn't have a makeup air inlet pipe in place, one can be easily added.

If opting to have a furnace or boiler replaced with a new, energy-efficient model, consider paying more for a high-efficiency sealed combustion unit. These systems draw combustion air directly from outside the house. This eliminates the need for a lot of makeup air, though the need to supply a gas- or oil-fired water heater may still be there.

burning appliances with a source of makeup air, the air may be drawn from other less desirable pathways. One of these might be the water heater's flue pipe.

This problem might arise when a water heater and furnace happen to operate at the same time. Both demand makeup air. If not enough air is freely available, the furnace can draw its makeup air from the water heater's flue pipe. Should this occur, combustion by-products created by the water heater are vented back down the flue pipe and into the house. This condition is called "backdrafting," and it has potentially dangerous consequences.

Install Carbon Monoxide Detectors

Carbon monoxide found in the house environment can result from improperly burning and venting fuel-burning heating equipment, such as furnaces, boilers, space heaters, and fireplaces. It can also come from gas or oil water heaters, gas ranges, clothes dryers, and even automobile exhaust that leaks or is drawn into the house from an attached garage.

To raise an alert to the possibility that backdrafting or another problem is occurring, every house should have carbon-monoxide (CO) detectors installed. Smoke detectors are required in all homes, but in many parts of the country CO detectors are not required. Costing as little as $40, CO detectors signal a potentially dangerous buildup of the colorless, odorless, and tasteless gas.

The usual recommendation is that a CO detector be placed in or near the sleeping quarters in a house. The alarm will awaken the home's occupants if the detector picks up the presence of the gas. It is a good idea to also place a second detector in or near a home's mechanical room. Venting malfunction is most likely to occur in this area. Municipal fire departments often have programs that give smoke detectors away for free. Some are starting to do the same with CO detectors.

Replacing Windows Can Result in Humidity Problems

After some types of energy upgrading have been done in homes, many people have observed that conditions inside their homes have changed markedly, especially during the winter. A common scenario is that after a homeowner has replaced old windows with new ones, excess moisture begins to appear inside the house—notably condensation on cold mornings on the inside panes of the new window glass. What happened?

Old windows are usually not airtight. They allow air to infiltrate the house and also to leave the house. This sets up an uncontrolled ventilation pattern that removes moisture from inside the house (in the form of water vapor) and imports dry air from outside. The result is that dry air enters the home during most of the winter, which is a common complaint from those who live in leaky older homes.

Once the old, leaky windows are replaced with airtight new ones, indoor moisture no longer has an easy means of escape. It builds up to levels that can create condensation on cold surfaces. Since window glazing is usually the coldest surface in most houses, that's where the condensation shows up first. Customers who thought having new windows installed would rid them of condensation on their windows sometimes find just the opposite to be the case. They're getting more condensation than ever.

The new windows are not at fault. There is simply too much humidity in the house. The solution is to reduce the humidity level inside. After that, the condensation is reduced or disappears. Homeowners who undertake comprehensive air sealing in their homes often find similar problems with moisture buildup. They've cut off the ventilation that diluted the humidity and brought in drier air from outside.

Similarly, an upgrade to sealed combustion furnaces and boilers can lead to issues with excess humidity. The problem lies in the fact that drier outdoor air that used to be drawn into the house by the combustion process is no longer streaming inside. The air inside the house is not being replaced with outdoor air. Humid air that was formerly diluted with the incoming drier air is now predominant, and condensation difficulties can crop up.

Provide Adequate Ventilation to Ensure Good Air Quality

In the absence of sufficient air exchange with the outdoors, indoor air can start to suffer quality problems. Odors from cooking and pets, off-gassing from building materials and furnishings, radon gas, combustion by-products from gas ranges, and other pollutants can accumulate. Studies reveal that, because we spend approximately 90 percent of our time indoors, exposure to these items can be dangerous, especially for children, seniors, and those who suffer from cardiovascular or respiratory diseases. The solution is to increase ventilation in order to dilute and exhaust the problem air.

Provide Source-Control Ventilation

One good way to reduce humidity and air pollutants is to attack the problem at the source. Because bathroom fans reduce the level of indoor humidity by venting water vapor to the outside, turn on the fan when bathing or showering. Turn on the fan to a kitchen range hood while cooking to vent odors and humidity. This is especially important with a gas range or oven. Gas ranges produce combus-

HEAT RECOVERY VENTILATORS

For homes with chronic indoor air quality problems that can't be eliminated or reduced by manual ventilation and removing the pollutants and humidity at the source, other means are available to introduce fresh air with minimal heat loss. Heat recovery ventilators (HRVs) use fans to continually bring in air from outside the house. As incoming air enters the HRV, it passes through a heat exchanger that is kept warm by the indoor air exiting the other side. Because the two airstreams never mix, the only thing transferred from the outgoing airstream to the incoming one is heat. While there is not a 100-percent heat transfer, the exchange is efficient enough that the home's heating system can quickly warm the incoming fresh air.

An HRV can be installed either as a stand-alone system or tied into forced-air furnace ducting. The fans, used to pull in and push out the air, are small, but they do use some electricity. Filters can be added to the installation in order to clean the incoming air before it enters the house. A correctly installed HRV should be virtually unnoticeable to the homeowner. There should be little or no noise, and the mix of incoming air with the air already inside the house should not create drafts or cold spots. An HRV can also be shut off when it is not needed.

tion by-products that collect in the house unless vented. Recirculating-type range hoods are somewhat effective at removing airborne grease, but they do not take combustion by-products out of the air. An outside-venting hood is the better choice.

Air Filtration and Whole-House Ventilation

Air filters, either stand-alone or furnace-mounted, can be helpful in straining solid matter like dust and dead skin cells (from both humans and pets) from the air, but they are not effective at removing gas-type pollutants.

One method of reducing the level and impact of indoor air pollutants and excess humidity is to mix the indoor air with fresh, dry air from outside the house. But after spending hours and dollars trying to increase the airtightness of the house in order to make it more energy-efficient, how do you increase the ventilation without reducing the effect of the changes just accomplished?

It is difficult to make an older home so airtight that indoor air pollution becomes a major problem—or at least one that can't be solved by taking one or two simple steps to alleviate the condition. Old houses just have too many places where air can leak out (and outdoor air can be drawn in). It is impossible find and plug them all. Newer homes are generally more airtight from the start.

If a house feels stale, stuffy, or excessively humid, simply opening a door or window for a few minutes each day will replace some of the bad air with fresh air. Homeowners with children may find that this process takes place naturally, as incoming and outgoing traffic continually pumps air in and out of the house. If it does become necessary to occasionally ventilate by opening doors and windows, the heat loss will be minimal if they aren't left open for too long a period.

Ice Dams on a Roof Indicate Energy Inefficiency

Ice dams on a roof in the winter are the end result of heat escaping the house and leaking into the attic, which indicates energy inefficiency. Ice dams are the result of poor air sealing, a lack of insulation, and inadequate ventilation in an attic.

Warm air travels upward because of its natural buoyancy. As it reaches the ceiling in the top floor, it seeks ways to rise even higher through cracks and gaps in the ceiling and walls. Some of those pathways are obvious; many others are not. As discussed in earlier chapters, openings around and through recessed canister lights, whole-house fan installations, attic-access hatchways and pull-down stairs, and electrical boxes in the ceiling and walls all provide conduits from the house into the attic. Moreover, heat is conducted upward through the top-floor ceiling through inadequate attic floor insulation. The result of the air leaks and conducted heat is an accumulation of warm air in the attic.

When snow falls on a roof, it acts as insulation, protecting the roof surface from the outside cold air. The combination of heat from below and snow on top creates conditions that warm the roof sheathing and shingles.

Warm shingles melt the snow lying on them. The resulting water runs down the roof under the snowpack. As it reaches the roof edge, there is no longer any heat from below to warm the shingles and sustain the melting process. The water freezes along the overhangs and starts to build into ice dams.

As the ice dams build up higher over the course of the winter, due to the constantly melting snow on the roof, water starts to form ponds behind the dams. Eventually, if the water level gets high enough and if the roof is inadequately protected from water intrusion, it starts to seep in underneath the shingles. In the worst cases, water can penetrate into the soffit areas, get behind the siding, and even enter the house through the interior ceilings and walls. Ice dams can be extremely destructive, and they result in millions of dollars in insurance claims every year.

Air Sealing, Insulation, and Ventilation Can Stop Ice Dams

The root cause of ice dams is excess heat in the attic. Undertaking the air sealing and insulating measures described earlier in this book will help reduce the heat leakage problem. The idea is to make the attic as cold as possible—as cold as the outside air—to reduce or eliminate the snow melting that starts the ice dam formation process. Ventilation through the attic also exhausts any heat that does manage to make it up there.

An ideal attic ventilation scheme involves several components: soffit vents that introduce air into the attic under the eave edges; air channels—that is, chutes that hold insulation back from the underside of the roof sheathing and direct the air upward from the soffits into the attic; and high roof or ridge vents that convey the air to the outdoors.

The chutes are important because insulation lying against the underside of the roof sheathing forms a thermal bridge that allows heat from the house below to travel through the insulation directly to the sheathing. It is essential to break that thermal bridge to eliminate the direct conveyance of the heat to the sheathing and also to promote the free flow of air into the rest of the attic from the soffit vents.

Attic ventilation is also needed to reduce moisture concentration in the attic environment. Air that travels into the attic from the house below carries water vapor. Unless that moisture is vented away, it can condense on the cold insulation, framing, and sheathing. If allowed to continue, the wet surroundings can create conditions conducive to mildew and mold growth, and even to rotting.

Adequate attic ventilation also pays off in the summer. Air flowing through the soffit vents and up through the ridge or high roof vents exhausts heat. Venting the attic means less heat is transferred downward through the attic floor insulation and into the house below. A cooler attic means the A/C doesn't have to run as often, which conserves energy dollars.

Comprehensive air sealing, insulation, and ventilation can reduce or eliminate the formation of ice dams on your house roof in the winter while paying dividends in the summer. Plus, this type of energy-saving upgrading is a onetime event in the life of the house. Add vents, do the air sealing, add insulation, and never worry about it again.

CONTRACTING

Hiring a Contractor for Work on Energy Upgrading

An oft-repeated general recommendation is to get at least three estimates from contractors to do any type of work on a home. In some areas that is difficult to accomplish. Either there aren't many contractors around who do a particular type of work, or it may be difficult deciding exactly whom to call from a long list. Consequently, many homeowners ask around at their workplaces, churches, schools, or at social gatherings for the names of contractors who have done similar work for their neighbors, friends, or colleagues.

Recommendations from others are often successful because those contacts can describe the manner in which the contractor conducted himself or herself while on the job. A contractor who did satisfactory work for one client, however, might not perform as well for another, and the perception of that contractor might also vary from client to client.

Hiring out contracting work is in many ways risky. It is difficult to ascertain the quality of the work until the job is complete. The scope and timing of the job can change along the way; there might be personality conflicts with the people hired to do the work; or the workers might find something that was not anticipated in the job that costs more money to

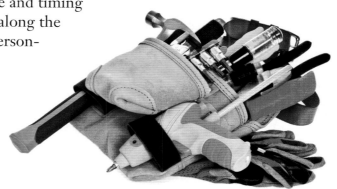
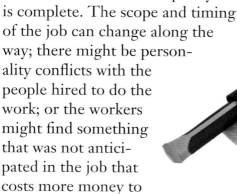

remedy. Anything can happen between signing the initial contact and the final billing.

To increase the odds of a successful encounter with a contractor, do some homework first.

The initial task is to find out from the local building department or state building regulation office what licenses and qualifications are necessary for a contractor to do the type of work needed. Also ask about insurance requirements. Many homeowners have been unpleasantly surprised to learn that if a worker is injured on a job site and is not covered under a contractor's workers' compensation policy, the homeowner—or the homeowner's insurance company—is responsible for the injured party.

Be sure the contractor has the proper regulatory qualifications, licenses, and insurance in place before considering him or her for a job. Because contractors are used to being asked for documentary paperwork, those who have their bases covered with respect to these questions will have the necessary documents on hand.

After narrowing down the search to three or four candidates, try to meet with each. Long projects or disruptive ones require very close contact between the homeowner and contractor. If one doesn't seem to be a good fit, interview another. A good working relationship will make all the difference.

Get All Contract Information in Writing

Once comfortable with a contractor, be sure any estimates for the work are written down, along with a comprehensive summary of the scope of the work, material specifications, and a timetable. Some homeowners request clauses in a contract that penalize the contractor for each day the job is unfinished after a set date—though these are usually reserved for larger projects that might take months to complete.

Be sure each party understands the part he or she will play in the work process. Communication between a contractor and a homeowner is vital for work to proceed smoothly toward a successful conclusion.

There should be a payment schedule included in the final contract. It is not unusual for a contractor to ask for a portion of the money up front in order to get started on the job. Such payments are negotiable, though the contractor might have a set percentage that he or she always works with. Be sure the contract reserves the right to withhold final payment until the job has been satisfactorily completed as specified.

Hiring someone to work on a home is daunting at first. But the more time and effort put into gathering information, the better the project will turn out. Therefore, be prepared to ask pertinent questions up front. Millions of homeowners hire contractors to do work on their homes each year, and the majority of those jobs turn out satisfactorily for both parties. The ones that do not, however, often make headlines—much to the detriment of the bulk of honest, hardworking, and knowledgeable contractors.

WHILE AWAY

Save Energy While the House Is Vacant

If leaving home for more than a couple of days, reduce the utility bill—and also protect the house—by doing a few simple things before walking out the door.

First, unplug any appliances that don't need to be on, including the TV, VCR, DVD player, the cable box, computers and their peripherals, stereo systems, and the microwave oven. All of these devices use electricity even when they're off. They also can be harmed by power surges and nearby lighting strikes. Plus, electrical items can short-circuit and cause fires (though rarely). If these devices are plugged into a power strip, unplug the power strip to completely terminate connection to the electrical power grid.

On a gas water heater, turn the thermostat dial to the "Vacation" setting. That setting still keeps the pilot light lit, but the burner won't fire to keep the tank full of hot water. Mark the dial before turning it down so it will be easy to dial it back up to its former setting. For an electric water heater, flip the disconnect or breaker to shut off its power at the main service panel.

Shut off the water to the house at the main shut-off valve and open a faucet or two in order to relieve pressure in the pipes. The hoses on clothes washers burst with surprising regularity, and if this happens when the house is unoccupied, the basement could fill up with water. In addition, the house will be protected in the winter should a power failure occur when it is cold enough inside the house to freeze water in the pipes.

Turn the thermostat down as far as it will go in the winter—most can drop to 55 degrees. In the summer, just turn the thermostat to "off." Why heat or cool a house when no one is around to benefit?

Put a couple of lights on timers, set to run an hour or two at night in order to make the house look occupied.

Finally, make friends with the neighbors so they can look in on the house every day or so. There's no substitute for a set of eyes watching over a house while it is unoccupied.